D1228721

WITHDRAWN

LONDON PUBLIC LIBRARY
20 EAST FIRST STREET
LONDON, OHIO 43140

11/05

This Is Your Government™

THE DEPARTMENT OF COMMERCE

Jan Goldberg

rosen
central™

The Rosen Publishing Group, Inc., New York

This book is dedicated to the memory of my beloved mother and father, Sam and Sylvia Lefkovitz, and to my beloved aunt and uncle, Fay and Harry Nesker.

Published in 2006 by The Rosen Publishing Group, Inc.
29 East 21st Street, New York, NY 10010

Copyright © 2006 by The Rosen Publishing Group, Inc.

First Edition

All rights reserved. No part of this book may be reproduced in any form without permission in writing from the publisher, except by a reviewer.

Library of Congress Cataloging-in-Publication Data

Goldberg, Jan.
The Department of Commerce / by Jan Goldberg.—1st ed.
    v. cm.—(This is your government)
Includes bibliographical references and index.
Contents: The history of the Department of Commerce—The Secretaries of Commerce—How the Department of Commerce works—The Department of Commerce in the twenty-first century.
ISBN 1-4042-0207-2 (lib. bdg.)
ISBN 1-4042-0660-4 (pbk. bdg.)
1. United States. Dept. of Commerce—Juvenile literature. 2. United States—Commercial policy. 3. Industrial policy—United States. [1. United States. Dept. of Commerce. 2. Industrial policy.]
I. Title. II. Series.
HF73.U5G65 2005
381'.0973—dc22
                                                                2003027574

Manufactured in the United States of America

On the cover: From left to right: George B. Cortelyou, William C. Redfield, Juanita M. Kreps, Ronald H. Brown, and Carlos M. Gutierrez.

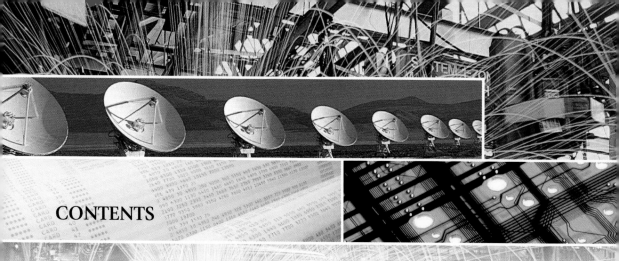

CONTENTS

Introduction

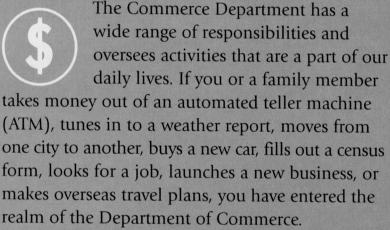

The Commerce Department has a wide range of responsibilities and oversees activities that are a part of our daily lives. If you or a family member takes money out of an automated teller machine (ATM), tunes in to a weather report, moves from one city to another, buys a new car, fills out a census form, looks for a job, launches a new business, or makes overseas travel plans, you have entered the realm of the Department of Commerce.

The department's purpose is to encourage foreign and domestic commerce and to support the efforts of American businesses. Its goals include encouraging the nation's economic growth, creating jobs, and improving living standards for all Americans.

The Department of Commerce is a cabinet-level government office, and the secretary of commerce is

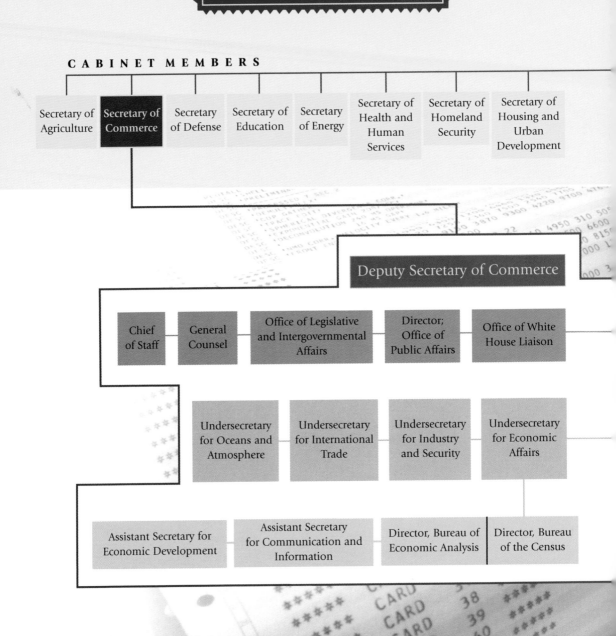

Department of Commerce Organization Chart

CABINET MEMBERS

- Secretary of Agriculture
- Secretary of Commerce
- Secretary of Defense
- Secretary of Education
- Secretary of Energy
- Secretary of Health and Human Services
- Secretary of Homeland Security
- Secretary of Housing and Urban Development

Deputy Secretary of Commerce

- Chief of Staff
- General Counsel
- Office of Legislative and Intergovernmental Affairs
- Director; Office of Public Affairs
- Office of White House Liaison

- Undersecretary for Oceans and Atmosphere
- Undersecretary for International Trade
- Undersecretary for Industry and Security
- Undersecretary for Economic Affairs

- Assistant Secretary for Economic Development
- Assistant Secretary for Communication and Information
- Director, Bureau of Economic Analysis
- Director, Bureau of the Census

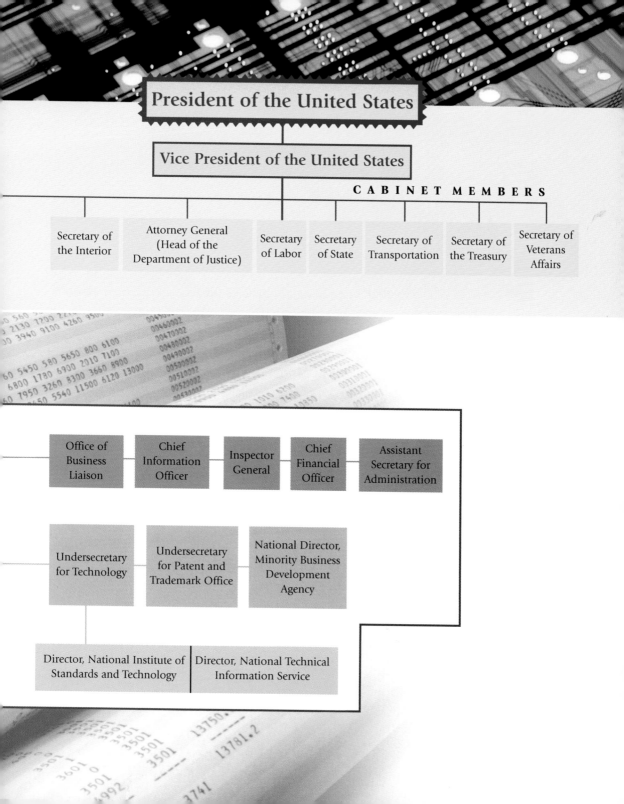

President of the United States

Vice President of the United States

CABINET MEMBERS

| Secretary of the Interior | Attorney General (Head of the Department of Justice) | Secretary of Labor | Secretary of State | Secretary of Transportation | Secretary of the Treasury | Secretary of Veterans Affairs |

Office of Business Liaison

Chief Information Officer

Inspector General

Chief Financial Officer

Assistant Secretary for Administration

Undersecretary for Technology

Undersecretary for Patent and Trademark Office

National Director, Minority Business Development Agency

Director, National Institute of Standards and Technology

Director, National Technical Information Service

A National Oceanic and Atmospheric Administration (NOAA) P-3 plane flies into the eye of a hurricane to take measurements on its wind strength, speed, direction, and moisture content. The National Weather Service is an office within NOAA, which in turn is part of the Department of Commerce.

a cabinet-level position. This means that the secretary is directly appointed by the president of the United States, with the advice and consent, or agreement, of the U.S. Senate. Once appointed, the secretary of commerce enters the president's circle of advisers and keeps the president informed on all commerce issues. As head of the Department of Commerce, the secretary also puts the president's decisions concerning business and trade into effect.

Let's have a look at the history, many responsibilities, and future of the Department of Commerce, an agency that has a substantial effect on all of our lives.

CHAPTER ONE

The History of the Department of Commerce

The story of the Department of Commerce is a long and complicated one with many twists and turns. To better understand how it came into being, evolved, and grew into the enormous—and enormously important—cabinet department we know today, let's start at the very beginning.

Theodore Roosevelt

Following a stock market crash in 1893 and an economic downturn that lasted much of the last decade of the nineteenth century, Americans became more interested in reining in "big business"—the huge trusts and monopolies that were blamed for much of the country's economic woes. At the same

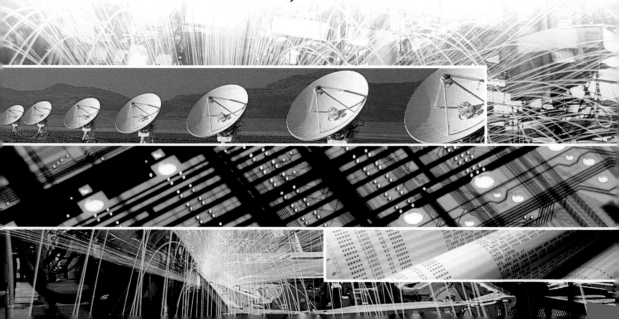

time, Americans wanted to see the enormous potential of U.S. industry put to greater use. American manufacturers agreed. The National Association of Manufacturers urged the U.S. government to form a Department of Commerce and Industry to monitor the health of the economy and ensure good business practices. Instead, in 1898, Congress created the U.S. Industrial Commission, which was responsible for investigating the nation's economic and social problems.

Though not what American manufacturers had asked for, the Industrial Commission did seem to help revitalize the economy. By 1900, the value of manufactured products in the United States was four times the value of the nation's agricultural products. Agriculture had been the leading American industry through much of the nineteenth century. Thanks in part to President William McKinley's efforts to encourage the sale of manufactured goods to other countries, the value of American exports almost tripled. For the first time in the nation's history, the United States sold more goods to other countries than it bought from them.

To keep this momentum going and to avoid a return to an economic slump, Theodore Roosevelt, who became president in September 1901 following McKinley's assassination, argued for the creation of a cabinet-level Department of Commerce and Labor. On February 14, 1903, Congress approved the legislation that would create the new department. Later on the very same day, President Roosevelt signed the bill creating the Department of Commerce and Labor—the first new executive department since the Civil War (1861–1865). Two days later, Roosevelt nominated his personal secretary, George B. Cortelyou, as the nation's first secretary of commerce and labor.

The Department of Commerce and Labor

After serving only one year as commerce and labor secretary, George B. Cortelyou left in 1904 to take charge of Theodore Roosevelt's campaign for reelection. Victor H. Metcalf, a California congressman, assumed the duties of the office next and served from July 1904 until December 1906. Oscar S. Straus, who had served as a United States ambassador to Turkey, was the next man named to this post. He served as secretary of commerce and labor until March 1909 when Roosevelt left office. Charles Nagel, a former Missouri Supreme Court justice, served as secretary from March 1909 until Congress divided the Department of Commerce and Labor into two separate offices in March 1913.

During the ten-year period that the Department of Commerce and Labor existed, it played a crucial part in expanding the markets for the United States' rapidly growing manufacturing sectors. In 1905, the Bureau of Manufactures was added to the department. Its mission was to focus on finding foreign markets for American products. By 1912, manufactured goods amounted to 47 percent of all U.S.

exports. This was the first year that the total value of exports exceeded the $1 billion mark.

Commerce and Labor Part Ways

The Department of Commerce and Labor was founded on the idea that a single government body could serve both industry and labor and help bosses and workers resolve their disagreements. This might have sounded like a reasonable idea in theory, but it soon became obvious that the conflicting interests of labor and business could not be fairly represented and resolved by the same department. Labor unions began to pressure the president to split the Department of Commerce and Labor into two separate departments, one to oversee the nation's industries and businesses, the other to serve and protect the people employed by those businesses. On March 4, 1913, on his very last day in office, President William Howard Taft signed legislation that divided the Department of Commerce and Labor into two individual cabinet-level departments. From this day on, the Department of Commerce had a single, clear focus—to encourage and develop U.S. industry and promote American products at home and abroad.

The First Secretary of Commerce

On March 15, 1913, Taft's successor, President Woodrow Wilson, named William C. Redfield as the first secretary of commerce.

THE DEPARTMENT OF COMMERCE AT WORK: THE CENSUS BUREAU

In 1951, the results of the U.S. Census were counted and recorded by computer—the UNIVAC I—for the first time in history.

Because it collects, studies, and publishes an enormous amount of information on the American population, the Census Bureau has long been at the forefront of data processing technology. Although census data were originally recorded with pen and paper, satellite technology may soon become the standard way for census takers to count Americans every ten years. By the turn of the last century, the Census Bureau had introduced punch cards and electric tabulating machines and sorters to help record and compile the information gathered by census takers. In 1951, the punch cards were replaced by the UNIVAC I, the first electronic computer used by a civilian government agency. The 1950s also saw the introduction of optical-sensing machines that could "read" and record the darkened circles that represented answers on completed

(continued on next page)

13

THE DEPARTMENT OF COMMERCE AT WORK: THE CENSUS BUREAU

(continued from preceding page)

questionnaires. In 2010, after the U.S. population will have more than tripled since the census of 1900, the Census Bureau hopes to give census takers mobile computers with global positioning system (GPS) receivers. These receivers, linked up with a GPS satellite that relays housing and geographic information, will allow census takers to locate streets, address ranges, and specific houses and apartments quickly and easily.

Redfield was a former congressman and New York businessman involved in mining, banking, insurance, and manufacturing.

In addition to his interest in finding new markets for American goods overseas, Secretary Redfield also wanted to harness the latest scientific advances to boost American productivity. He was convinced that U.S. manufacturers were not using technology to their best advantage. As a result, he actively supported the expansion of the Bureau of Standards. This office within the Department of Commerce was responsible for working with government, universities, and industry to encourage research and development in industry technologies, and to apply the results of the research toward improvements in the manufacturing of products.

Secretary Redfield resigned in October 1919, and President Wilson appointed Joshua W. Alexander as his successor. When Republican president Warren G. Harding took office seventeen months later, Alexander, a congressman from Missouri, resigned his position.

Herbert C. Hoover

The man President Harding appointed as secretary of commerce in March 1921 was an engineer named Herbert C. Hoover. Even as government spending declined, Hoover managed to persuade Congress to increase the department's appropriation (a sort of allowance) from $860,000 in 1920 to more than $5 million in 1928. When Hoover's term in office was over, he had increased the staff in the Department of Commerce to more than five times what it had been before his arrival.

While in office, Hoover's goal was to expand American commerce with foreign countries by increasing productivity and putting into practice new and improved business methods. He also wanted to turn the Department of Commerce into one of the most important and powerful agencies within the federal government.

Prosperous Times

By the late 1920s, economists began to notice an important new trend in the United States economy—the beginning of a shift in the workforce from manufacturing occupations to jobs in retail sales and professional and personal services (which would include such diverse services as health care, plumbing, and hairdressing). The Department of Commerce also noted another trend in its annual report for 1928. Besides those directly involved in the actual making of automobiles, 3 million additional American workers owed their livelihoods to the nation's growing fleet of cars, trucks, and buses. These included car salesmen, gas station attendants, road builders, commercial truck operators, and taxi and bus drivers.

Overall, the United States enjoyed prosperity during the administrations of Presidents Warren Harding and Calvin Coolidge. American families' income and business productivity increased considerably in a short period of time. Prices for farm products were rising. Americans began to believe their economy—and their nation—was invincible and would never again pass through hard times. This vote of confidence in the American economy was extended also to the nation's secretary of commerce, who was given much of the credit for the prosperity of the postwar years. In 1928, Herbert Hoover was elected president of the United States.

The Great Depression and the New Deal

Only eleven months later, however, on October 29, 1929, the good times of the 1920s came to a sudden halt with the most devastating stock market crash in American history. The steep

During the Great Depression, many Americans were suddenly thrown into desperate poverty and hunger. Breadlines formed and soup kitchens opened their doors in an attempt to keep the poorest from starvation. In this Depression-era photo, men line up around the block for a five-cent meal.

economic decline that followed for more than a decade, called the Great Depression, had an enormous effect on huge numbers of Americans, many of whom lost their jobs, their fortunes, and their savings.

By 1932, the national income had decreased by more than one-half from its 1929 level. Trade with foreign nations reached its lowest point since the Department of Commerce was created in 1913, as American exports fell by 34 percent and imports fell by 37 percent. Between 1929 and 1933, an astounding 125,000 businesses failed. In 1933, 14 million Americans (25 percent of all workers) were unemployed. The country was in a severe crisis, and pressure on the president and secretary of commerce to do something to pull the nation out of it was intense.

When Franklin Delano Roosevelt was elected to the presidency in 1932, his administration was charged with the responsibility of initiating some programs to improve economic conditions. Many of these programs, known collectively as the New Deal, were placed under the direction of the Department of Commerce, now led by Roosevelt's appointee, Daniel C. Roper. The programs stressed the creation of jobs and building projects that would lead to long-term economic health.

One New Deal program with which the Department of Commerce became closely associated was the National Recovery Administration (NRA). The NRA was responsible for putting into place the recommendations of the 1933 National Industrial Recovery Act. This act was designed to improve the economy by encouraging fair and orderly competition in business. Among other things, the act resulted in a maximum-hour workday and a minimum wage for American workers.

World War II

As President Roosevelt's New Deal policies began to put Americans back to work and the country began to pull itself out of the Great Depression, a world war began brewing in Europe. The Department of Commerce found its attention and energies divided between nurturing the American economy and preparing the nation for a massive war effort.

This poster from c. 1942 illustrates just how important American commerce and industry was to the war effort during World War II. Many factories that used to make cars, canned goods, or toys before the war were transformed into plants that could roll out guns, ammunition, bombs, jeeps, tanks, and airplanes for use overseas.

Following the Japanese attack on the American naval base at Pearl Harbor, Hawaii, on December 7, 1941, the United States declared war on Japan and entered World War II, three years after fighting between the Axis powers (Japan, Germany, and Italy) and the Allies (Russia, Great Britain, and France) had first begun. The Department of Commerce was called upon to help transform the country's peacetime industries into important supporters and suppliers of the war effort. For example, the Bureau of Standards developed uniform industrial standards to ensure that parts for various makes and models of guns, tanks, and aircraft be interchangeable. This would help boost supply and efficiency by making it easier to quickly produce very large quantities of important parts that could be used in several models of war equipment and weaponry.

The Department of Commerce also supervised the National Inventors Council, which helped identify and develop inventions that had potential military value. In addition, the department's various bureaus provided the United States military with maps, weather reports, and other information that was useful for planning battle strategy and troop movements.

From War to Peace

The Allies defeated the Axis powers in 1945, ending World War II. Though overjoyed by the return of peace, Europe was physically and economically devastated and in desperate need of help. In addition to the reconstruction of war-torn cities, the economies of European nations and Japan also had to be rebuilt. To aid foreign countries in rebuilding their economies, the Department of Commerce's Office of International Trade began working to encourage the importing of goods from abroad to the United States. Americans were also encouraged to travel overseas for vacations in order to pump more money into European economies.

The Department of Commerce assumed a key role in helping the American economy make the difficult transition from war to peace. An important part of this transition was the further opening up of the country through the building of roads. If more people and goods could move easily and quickly throughout the nation, then more money could be made.

By the early 1950s, following the transfer of the Bureau of Public Roads (in 1949) and the Maritime Administration (in 1950) to the Department of Commerce, the department became the federal government's principal transportation agency. In 1949, the department also established the Office of Transportation, which was responsible for coordinating transportation information and law. The nation's great interstate highway system was begun under the department's guidance in the 1950s. With the passage of the Interstate Highway Act in 1967, however, responsibility for the highway system was transferred to the newly created Department of Transportation.

The peacetime economy was also spurred by international trade. In 1956, Commerce Department officials assisted in renegotiating the General Agreement on Tariffs and Trade (GATT). This was an international accord between more than 100 countries that together account for more than 80 percent of world trade. GATT set up a code of conduct for governments in international trade and provides a forum for the settlement of trade disputes between nations that have signed the agreement. After many rounds of negotiation and revisions, GATT had substantially reduced tariffs (which are the taxes a nation places upon imports in order to give its own industries an advantage) and other barriers to free trade. GATT has since been replaced by the World Trade Organization (WTO).

The 1960s

As the United States headed into the 1960s, the Department of Commerce's efforts at home and abroad to stimulate the sale of American goods were showing signs of paying off nicely. In 1961, the department reported that world trade had reached a record high. At the same time, U.S. exports peaked at $19.9 billion and imports declined to $13.9 billion. This meant that the United States was selling more goods abroad than it was buying and more money was coming into its economy than going out.

Also in 1961, two additional programs designed to maintain the health of the U.S. economy were launched and would go on to become permanent fixtures of the Department of Commerce. The department initiated a pilot (test) project to stimulate development in economically depressed areas of the country, such as rural Appalachia and struggling inner cities. This program evolved into the Economic Development Administration, which was formally established in 1965.

The Commerce Department's second new program was the U.S. Travel Service, which became the U.S. Travel and Tourism Administration in 1981. It was created to promote the United States as a vacation destination for foreign tourists. By 1969, more than 1.5 million foreigners had visited the country, an increase of 230 percent from 1961. Foreign tourists had injected millions of dollars into local economies by visiting sites, buying souvenirs, staying in hotels, and eating in restaurants.

The 1970s

In the 1970s, the Department of Commerce continued to grow and develop new programs and offices that would expand the department's reach and influence in the American economy and the lives of the nation's citizens. In 1969, when President Richard M. Nixon appointed banker Maurice Stans as secretary of commerce, the department consisted of sixteen divisions with more than 25,000 employees.

Under Stans, the department reorganized and launched several new programs. One of these was the National Oceanic and Atmospheric Administration (NOAA), which was established in 1970. NOAA is a scientific agency responsible for weather forecasting, ocean charting, ocean research, and other related activities. NOAA consolidated the duties of various Commerce Department programs and five other agencies into one body.

In 1971, Nixon issued an executive order expanding the activities and programs of the Office of Minority Business Enterprise, a program created in 1969 to help minority-owned firms become established and succeed in business. In 1979, this office was renamed the Minority Business Development Agency (MBDA).

The 1980s

In the 1980s, under the leadership of Secretary of Commerce Malcolm Baldridge, the department became a major force in formulating national economic policy. It took a prominent role in supporting passage of the Export Trading Company Act of 1982, which was designed to encourage small- and medium-sized firms to enter into the export business. Baldridge also arranged trade conferences with the leaders of other nations. In 1982, President Ronald Reagan assigned the commerce secretary to lead a cabinet-level Trade Strike Force to investigate unfair trading practices and recommend corrective measures.

In 1987, Congress created the Bureau of Export Administration (BXA) within the Department of Commerce, giving it responsibility for national export-control policies that encouraged foreign trade while at the same time protecting national security. The new agency improved the enforcement of export laws and helped prevent the sale of sensitive goods (such as guns, missiles, or high-tech equipment) abroad that might end up in the hands of enemy nations and be used against the United States or its allies.

Into the Twenty-first Century

As the Department of Commerce entered the 1990s and the new millennium beyond, it was responsible for a wide and

THE DEPARTMENT OF COMMERCE AT WORK: THE ECONOMIC DEVELOPMENT ADMINISTRATION

In 2000, the Economic Development Administration (EDA) provided a $2 million grant to the Apollo Theater Restoration

The historic Apollo Theater in Harlem, New York

Company to help restore the Apollo Theater in Harlem, New York. Many legendary acts, including Ella Fitzgerald, James Brown, and Michael Jackson, got their start in this theater. The EDA hoped that by restoring the Apollo it would become an even bigger draw for tourists and theatergoers. The more people who come to central Harlem to visit the Apollo, the more money will be spent in the surrounding neighborhood, helping to spur the revitalization of a once vibrant but currently struggling area. The EDA estimated that the restoration would create 200 jobs in the theater's neighborhood, as well as 1,000 related jobs in the surrounding area. The project is thought to be responsible for the nearby development of Harlem USA (a major shopping complex) and a large multiplex movie theater.

ever-expanding variety of programs. Throughout the 1990s, the department launched several initiatives through its various agencies, offices, and bureaus to accomplish the following goals:

- Ⓢ Increase community and regional economic development
- Ⓢ Boost exports to create jobs at home and keep American businesses competitive overseas
- Ⓢ Offer more effective export counseling and financial services to American businesses
- Ⓢ Rebuild marine fisheries and improve their economic and environmental health
- Ⓢ Publish more effective and timely trade, economic, and statistical information for use by other government agencies and private businesses
- Ⓢ Increase access to credit (such as loans) for minority-owned businesses

In 2003, the department celebrated its 100th birthday as a cabinet-level department. Since 1913, when the Department of Commerce was separated from the Department of Labor, the Commerce Department has grown to employ more than 36,000 people in thirteen major operating units with an annual budget of more than $5 billion. Despite this growth, the Commerce Department still remains the federal government's smallest cabinet-level department in terms of budget.

The Department of Commerce continues to try to create a healthy economy by encouraging the efforts of American businesses at home and abroad. Today, the department has five primary missions: increasing business and trade; improving the nation's technological competitiveness; protecting the environment and encouraging environmentally friendly commerce; improving economic development; and compiling, analyzing, and publishing statistical information that is valuable and useful to American businesses.

Although some of these mission areas are as old as the department itself, others are quite new. What they all have in common is that they are designed to assist the business community and the nation in meeting the economic and technological challenges that face the country today and those that will be encountered in the future.

CHAPTER TWO

The Secretaries of Commerce

The list of individuals who have served as secretary of commerce is a long and distinguished one. Some of these outstanding leaders came from the business community. Others served in government before being appointed. Among the secretaries of commerce, there have been a president and a vice president of the United States, two House representatives, one senator, one state governor, two state lieutenant governors, and an ambassador to the Soviet Union and Great Britain. Some secretaries have even held other cabinet positions before entering the Department of Commerce. Elliot L. Richardson (secretary from 1976 to 1977) had previously served as secretary of the Departments

George B. Cortelyou served as the nation's first secretary of commerce and labor (1903–1904) under President Theodore Roosevelt. He began his career as a law reporter and principal of schools in New York. His first job in public service was as a stenographer to President Grover Cleveland in 1895.

of Health, Education, Welfare, and Defense, as well as attorney general and a U.S. ambassador.

Here are some important "firsts" among the secretaries of commerce:

💲 The first secretary of commerce and labor was George B. Cortelyou (February 18, 1903–June 30, 1904), under President Theodore Roosevelt. He had also served as postmaster general under Roosevelt and went on to become secretary of the treasury.

💲 The first secretary of commerce was William C. Redfield (March 5, 1913–October 31, 1919), under President Woodrow Wilson. Redfield first worked at a company that made stationery, but later became involved in mining, manufacturing, banking, and life insurance. Redfield served as Brooklyn, New

York's commissioner of public works before winning a seat in Congress representing New York. After leaving government, Redfield moved back to New York to work in the fields of banking, investments, and insurance. During this period, he wrote *The New Industrial Day*, a book that argued for a more scientific approach to management in business.

($) Juanita M. Kreps was the first woman to serve in this office (January 23, 1977–October 31, 1979), under President Jimmy Carter. At the time of her appointment, she was the only economist to serve as secretary of commerce. She went on to be a professor of economics at Duke University and a vice president of the school.

($) Ronald H. Brown was the first African American secretary of commerce (January 22, 1993–April 3, 1996), under President Bill Clinton. Before taking office, he was a lawyer, negotiator, and chairman of the Democratic National Committee. Sadly, he died in a plane crash on an official trade mission to Bosnia and Croatia (both part of the former Yugoslavia) on April 3, 1996.

Let's take a closer look at some of the Department of Commerce's most interesting and accomplished secretaries.

Herbert Hoover

Born on August 10, 1874, the son of a Quaker blacksmith in the Iowa village of West Branch, Herbert Hoover was orphaned at the age of eight and sent to live with an uncle in Oregon. The uncle became wealthy, allowing Hoover to study mining engineering at California's Stanford University, from which he graduated in 1895.

After working as an engineer for a private company in China for several years, Hoover returned to the United States at the outbreak of World War I (1914–1918). He was appointed by President Woodrow Wilson to head the Food Administration. In this role, Hoover encouraged Americans to cut back on what they ate so that food could be sent overseas to help feed Allied troops. At the war's end, he headed the American Relief Administration and organized shipments of food for millions of starving people in central Europe and the Soviet Union.

In 1921, President Warren G. Harding appointed Hoover as his secretary of commerce. Hoover made important contributions to public policy and was an active member of both the Harding and the Coolidge administrations. His time at the Department of Commerce was busy and productive. He developed many new foreign markets for American products and developed projects at home in navigation, irrigation, and flood control. As chairman of the Colorado River Commission, he oversaw the negotiations between six western states that led to the building of the Hoover Dam.

Hoover oversaw a period of great change within the Commerce Department, change driven mainly by new technology and emerging industries. He added divisions to the Department

The Hoover Dam was a monumental construction project on the Colorado River at the Arizona-Nevada border that was carried out while America was in the grip of the Depression. It stands 726.4 feet (221.4 meters) tall and weighs 6.6 million tons. With the help of thousands of men, it took only five years to build.

of Commerce that dealt with the growing radio and aeronautics industries. In 1927, he even participated in the first demonstration of television. He successfully argued for the standard sizing of products like tires, paper, plumbing nuts and bolts, and window frames, which helped manufacturers and builders save money and time. Hoover was also interested in protecting the environment and encouraged conservation efforts in the Chesapeake Bay and Alaska fisheries, among other places.

Herbert Hoover was one of the modern era's first secretaries of commerce. He was one of the first secretaries to address the unique challenges, dangers, and opportunities of the technology-driven twentieth century, with its mass production, automation, airplanes, televisions, massive construction projects, and feats of engineering. He felt technology must serve humanity, not enslave it. No matter how mechanized and efficient the American economy would become, it must not leave anyone behind. Modern society must ensure that everyone is fed, clothed, housed, and employed. In this sense, Herbert Hoover, a forward-thinking man with a commitment to humanity, set the tone for the Department of Commerce in an often cold and bewildering modern age.

Henry A. Wallace

Henry A. Wallace served as secretary of commerce from March 2, 1945, to September 20, 1946, under Presidents Franklin D. Roosevelt and Harry S. Truman. He was born in Iowa in 1888 and was educated at Iowa State College. When his father, Henry C. Wallace, owner and editor of the influential agricultural magazine *Wallace's Farmer*, was appointed secretary of agriculture by President Warren G. Harding in 1921, Henry A. Wallace took over his father's editing duties at the magazine. Later, in 1933, Henry A. Wallace was appointed secretary of agriculture in his own right by Franklin Roosevelt.

Wallace gained national attention as head of the Agriculture Department, taking charge of the administration of the Agricultural Adjustment Agency (AAA) so successfully that

Roosevelt chose Wallace as his running mate in the successful reelection campaign of 1940. The AAA was a Depression-era agricultural program designed to both assist struggling American farmers and improve the health of the agricultural industry as a whole.

Though Wallace distinguished himself as a loyal, hard-working wartime vice president over the next four years, he failed to gain enough support from his own Democratic Party to remain on the ticket with Roosevelt during the reelection campaign of 1944. Wallace was seen as too liberal by his more conservative Democratic colleagues. Roosevelt wanted him to remain in the cabinet, however, and Wallace accepted his appointment as secretary of commerce in 1945. He remained at the Commerce Department until September 1946, when he was forced to resign for having publicly criticized President Harry Truman's aggressive foreign policy. Former vice president Truman had risen to the presidency following Roosevelt's death in April 1945.

After leaving the Commerce Department, Wallace returned to editing, but this time at the *New Republic*, a liberal news magazine. At the end of 1946, Wallace continued to campaign for liberal causes by helping to found the Progressive Citizens of America, a workers' group dedicated to peaceful relations with the Soviet Union.

As a result of his activities with the Progressive Citizens of America, Wallace was labeled a Communist sympathizer at a time when the Cold War was getting under way and Americans were increasingly afraid of the prospect of a Soviet-dominated world. After a failed presidential bid in 1948, Wallace retired from political life. He continued to write about politics and agriculture until his death in 1965.

William Averell Harriman

W. Averell Harriman served as secretary of commerce from October 7, 1946, to April 22, 1948, under President Harry S. Truman. He was born into a family fortune gained through the railroads, but he sought his own fortune in banking and shipbuilding before entering government. Under President Franklin D. Roosevelt, Harriman served as administrative officer to the National Recovery Administration (NRA) in 1934 and 1935, and he was an official in the Department of Commerce from 1937 to 1940. He was ambassador to the Soviet Union from 1943 to 1946. He was serving as ambassador to Great Britain in 1946 when President Truman appointed him to be his secretary of commerce.

After leaving the Department of Commerce, Harriman was sent abroad as a United States representative for the post–World War II European Recovery Program, also known as the Marshall Plan. The Marshall Plan offered American financial aid to European countries devastated by the war and in great need of physical and economic recovery.

Returning to the United States, he was later elected governor of New York, serving from 1955 to 1959, and was an unsuccessful candidate for the Democratic presidential nomination in 1956. Harriman became President John F. Kennedy's special roving ambassador in 1961. From 1965 to 1968, he was ambassador at large for Southeast Asian affairs under President Lyndon B. Johnson. When the 1968 Paris peace talks on Vietnam opened, he served as chief United States negotiator. Harriman is the author of *Peace with Russia*, published in 1959, and *America and Russia in a Changing World*, published in 1971. In 1978, he was appointed the senior member of the U.S. delegation to the United Nations General Assembly's Special Session on Disarmament. William Averell Harriman died in 1986.

Elliot Lee Richardson

Elliot Lee Richardson served as secretary of commerce from February 2, 1976, to January 20, 1977, under President Gerald Ford. He was born in Boston, Massachusetts, on July 20, 1920. Richardson graduated from Harvard University in 1941 and from Harvard Law School in 1947. A distinguished public servant, Richardson held several high-level positions in Massachusetts's state government, including secretary of health, education, and welfare, attorney general, and lieutenant governor. In Washington, D.C., he served as President Richard Nixon's secretary of defense and attorney general.

THE DEPARTMENT OF COMMERCE AT WORK: THE NATIONAL INSTITUTE OF STANDARDS AND TECHNOLOGY

Following the destruction of the World Trade Center on September 11, 2001, the National Institute of Standards and

Technology (NIST) launched a $16 million two-year investigation into why the structure of the Trade Center towers failed and then collapsed. The investigation's focus was to be on the buildings' construction, materials used, and the technical conditions that led to their collapse. The results of the investigation were to be used to help improve the safety of the nation's tall buildings, enhance fire safety, better protect those inside the buildings, and develop better emergency procedures. A sepa-

The World Trade Center spews smoke and flames after both its towers were struck by hijacked airliners on September 11, 2001.

rate series of NIST interviews with Trade Center survivors and rescue workers was also planned to learn more about the evacuation of the buildings and the emergency response and how to improve procedures for both.

Richardson is probably most recognized as the U.S. attorney general who served Republican President Nixon during the investigation into the Watergate break-in. The Watergate was an apartment and office complex that housed the headquarters of the Democratic National Committee. Members of Nixon's administration organized a break-in and bugging of the office, possibly in order to gather information on the Democrats' presidential campaign strategy, although the exact motive was never discovered. Though it was never proven that Nixon ordered the break-in, it did become clear that he engaged in a cover-up afterward.

In 1973, in the midst of the Watergate investigation, President Nixon ordered Richardson to fire the Watergate special prosecutor, Archibald Cox, a man Richardson himself had appointed. Instead of following Nixon's orders, Richardson chose to resign. After Nixon resigned the presidency in order to avoid impeachment (being brought up on charges by the U.S. Senate), Richardson served as President Gerald Ford's ambassador to Great Britain and secretary of commerce. Later, he accepted President Jimmy Carter's offer to become ambassador at large. Richardson died of complications from a cerebral hemorrhage on December 31, 1999. He remains to this day one of the few figures in Nixon's Watergate-era administration who commands respect and admiration for his courage and integrity.

CHAPTER THREE

How the Department of Commerce Works

Today's secretary of commerce oversees a diverse cabinet agency of 40,000 workers and a $5 billion budget. The Department of Commerce continues to focus on promoting and ensuring the economic health of American business, both at home and abroad. In addition, the department gathers vast amounts of economic and population data, issues patents and trademarks, helps set industrial standards, forecasts the weather, researches the oceans, and oversees the policy of the telecommunications industry, among many other responsibilities.

The commerce secretary works closely with the president and Congress in an attempt to preserve the United States'

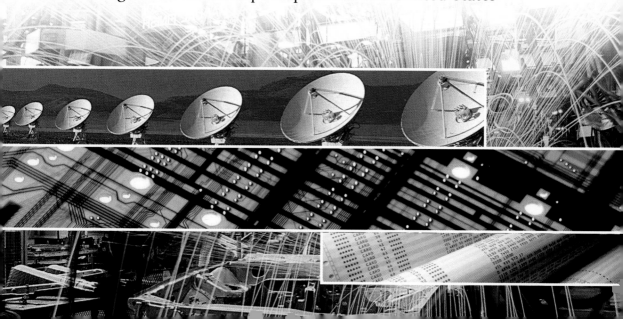

position as a leader in the global marketplace. The secretary is an important member of the president's economic team. He or she offers advice on many commerce-related issues, including trade, business concerns, energy policy, and overall United States economic policy. Secretaries also travel on trade missions to places like Russia, China, Mexico, Africa, and South America in order to promote American exports and open up new markets for American goods.

Because cutting-edge technologies are vital to the United States' continued status as one of the world's leading economic powers, today's Commerce Department focuses on developing more state-of-the-art technologies. It also promotes the expansion of e-commerce and telecommunications, and improves the department's economic data collection and distribution capabilities.

Today's Department of Commerce includes the following bureaus.

Bureau of Industry and Security

The Bureau of Industry and Security (BIS) is charged with advancing U.S. national security, foreign policy, and economic interests. Fulfilling this mission requires a wide range of activities. The BIS carefully regulates the export of sensitive goods and technologies that might be dangerous in the wrong hands, such as weaponry or nuclear power plant equipment. It also helps other countries with their export controls to ensure that dangerous goods do not spread around the globe. The BIS instructs American industries involved in the manufacture of weapons on how to follow the requirements of international arms control agreements. It also monitors the health and efficiency of the American defense industries, helping to guarantee that the nation does not become vulnerable to attack.

By encouraging the development of new technologies in the defense industry, the BIS tries to make sure that the United States does not lose its worldwide military superiority. The bureau strives to work cooperatively with private industries, other parts of the U.S. government, state and local governments, and other nations to maintain American security and prosperity and a safer world.

Economics and Statistics Administration

The Economics and Statistics Administration (ESA) is made up of the Bureau of Economic Analysis (BEA) and the Bureau of the Census. The BEA produces economic statistics that provide a sort of snapshot of the American economy and influence the decisions made by government officials, businesspeople, households, and individuals. The BEA prepares reports on the economic situation of specific regions and industries, as well as the nation at large. It also tracks the place the United States occupies within the global marketplace.

The Bureau of the Census—known as "the nation's fact finder"—conducts a nationwide census every ten years. A census is a thorough counting of the population, which often also collects personal information such as income, marital status, race, and age. This information allows the government and businesses to track changes in the population that may affect the American economy and the market for their goods and services. In addition to taking a census of the population every ten years (the most recent 2000 census counted 281.4 million Americans), the Census Bureau also conducts censuses of economic activity and state and local governments every five years.

Economic Development Administration

The Economic Development Administration (EDA) provides grants to economically struggling communities to help create jobs, preserve existing jobs, and encourage industrial and commercial growth. EDA investments also help create local businesses and pay for rebuilding efforts after natural disasters.

International Trade Administration

The International Trade Administration (ITA) is the lead unit for global trade in the Department of Commerce. Its mission is to promote United States products overseas and to fight against unfair competition or closed foreign markets. To

A representative of the Department of Commerce's Minority Business Development Agency (MBDA) assists a small-business owner who is seeking ways to stay competitive with larger and wealthier businesses. The MBDA encourages the creation and growth of minority-owned businesses in the United States, partly by providing business owners with important financing, marketing, and management tips.

achieve this goal, the ITA provides American businesses with information that helps them identify and gain access to foreign markets for their goods. To ensure that foreign markets remain open to American goods, the ITA enforces trade laws and agreements and works with other governments to settle any trade disputes.

Minority Business Development Agency

The Minority Business Development Agency (MBDA) promotes the creation, growth, and expansion of minority-owned businesses in the United States by providing minority business owners with such assistance as loans, important business information, and valuable management tips.

THE DEPARTMENT OF COMMERCE AT WORK: THE NATIONAL OCEANIC AND ATMOSPHERIC ADMINISTRATION

In addition to helping track and warn coastal communities and ships at sea about the approach of Hurricane Isabel in October 2003, the National Oceanic and Atmospheric Administration (NOAA) also helped protect ships and waterways after the powerful storm had passed by. Immediately after Isabel passed through North Carolina, Virginia, and Maryland, NOAA ships swung into action to survey the area's waterways and make sure that nothing was blocking them or otherwise posing a danger to ships traveling on them. A particular concern was shoaling—parts of a waterway that become very shallow following a big storm. Ships can easily become grounded or severely damaged in shallow water. Thanks to NOAA's immediate action, the area's ports and waterways were all reopened within only a few days of the storm, and business—such as shipping and commercial fishing—was again being conducted on the water.

National Oceanic and Atmospheric Administration

The National Oceanic and Atmospheric Administration (NOAA) is dedicated to protecting and learning more about the environment. It does this by gathering data on the world's oceans and atmosphere, the Sun, and outer space. This research can be used to develop policies and technologies that will allow us to both better use and better protect our oceans and coasts, the environment in general, and the fragile atmosphere that surrounds, protects, and sustains our planet. In addition, NOAA is able to warn of dangerous storms and short-term weather trends through the information it gathers from its satellites.

NOAA is part of the Department of Commerce because the nation's economic health—its ability to do business—is strongly affected by weather and climate. The ability to forecast accurately short- and long-term weather, climate, and environmental conditions is crucial to a wide range of business decisions, including such basic ones as where to do business; what products to make, grow, or harvest; and how to get goods to market.

National Telecommunications and Information Administration

The National Telecommunications and Information Administration (NTIA) is the Commerce Department agency that is responsible for advising the president on all domestic and international telecommunications and information technology issues. Radios, telephones, televisions, computers, and the Internet are all forms of telecommunication. The way in which information or content—such as a television show, a

The convenience of placing a call from almost anywhere, at any time fueled the popularity of cell phones. Now, they can do even more. The one shown here can show maps of local streets, indicating museums, restaurants, amusement parks, hotels, and other attractions. It can also receive Internet service. Other cell phones take digital photographs. The Commerce Department seeks to bolster the economy, create jobs, and spur product sales by encouraging this kind of innovation in the telecommunications industry.

phone call, an e-mail, or a Web site—is broadcast, posted, or delivered and then viewed, read, or used by consumers is known as information technology.

The NTIA seeks to encourage innovation and competition in the telecommunications industries in order to create jobs and provide consumers with new high-quality products (like cell phones and digital television) and services (like long-distance phone service and Internet access) at lower prices. Some specific NTIA goals include the providing of all Americans with affordable phone and cable service. This ensures that rural and economically troubled urban areas have access to advanced telecommunications technology, such as Internet access. Another NTIA goal is to provide public radio and television broadcasters with hardware that allows them to extend their broadcast reach. This encourages the development of new telecommunications technologies. It also opens up foreign markets for American telecommunications products and services.

Office of the Inspector General

The Office of the Inspector General ensures that the Department of Commerce works as hard and as effectively as it can for American business and the American people by watching over department activities. Its mission is to detect any fraud, waste, abuse, or violations of the law occurring within the department. To encourage the greatest possible efficiency and effectiveness in department operations, the Office of the Inspector General conducts investigations and reviews each bureau within the Department of Commerce.

Patent and Trademark Office

The Patent and Trademark Office (PTO) provides patents to inventors and trademark protection to businesses that develop new and innovative products. A patent is an official document that states that an inventor has the exclusive right for a certain period of time to make, use, or sell his or her invention. A trademark states that the owner of a product (whether an individual or a company) is the only one allowed to make and sell it.

Through patents and trademarks, the PTO encourages the development of new products and technologies. The issuing of patents encourages inventors to commit the time, energy, and money necessary to create something new and innovative because they know they will be able to protect, control, and sell their invention or idea. A patent will prevent their idea from being stolen and copied by competitors who would profit from the inventor's hard work. Businesses often invest millions of dollars in developing experimental and untested products because they know that once the product is trade-marked, only they will be able to manufacture and sell it. This will allow them to cover their research and development costs and eventually make a profit.

Technology Administration

The Technology Administration (TA) seeks to spur the economy, create high-paying jobs, and improve the health of the environ-ment by encouraging technological and industrial innovation. To encourage this innovation, the TA, through its National Technical Information Service, provides public access to government-funded scientific, technical, engineering, and business-related information.

CHAPTER FOUR

The Department of Commerce in the Twenty-first Century

As the Department of Commerce heads into the twenty-first century, its strategies, activities, and programs will need to adapt to changing global conditions and challenges. The political, economic, technological, and security environment that exists today is substantially different from that of only a decade ago. It can be expected that the world will again look very different another few decades from now. The Department of Commerce must try to anticipate what the world will look like in the near future and begin preparing for it immediately. Otherwise, the United States could lose its position in the world as an economic, military, and political leader.

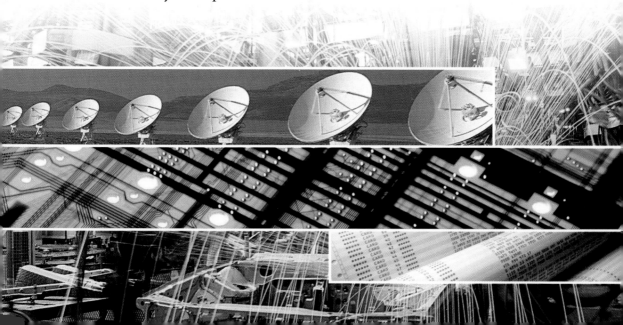

A protester opposed to the World Trade Organization (WTO) and its globalization and free trade policies states his opinion in 1999 during a WTO meeting in Seattle, Washington. WTO protesters believe that free trade really means increasing corporate control of the world. Instead, they feel that the citizens of each country should be involved in business decisions that affect their health, environment, work, and society.

These are just a few of the areas likely to be of great concern to the Department of Commerce in the twenty-first century.

Free Trade

The Department of Commerce is likely to continue to press for the opening of foreign markets to American goods and services and the lowering of barriers to trade, such as tariffs or subsidies. The North American Free Trade Act went into effect in 1994, creating open markets among Canada, Mexico, and the United States. The Department of Commerce will probably argue for the extension of the free trade zone to Central and South America and the entire Western Hemisphere. The department will also seek, through international organizations like the World Trade Organization, to further open markets in Europe and Asia and establish greater trade with potentially huge markets like China. While encouraging greater international trade, however, the Department of Commerce must continue to ensure that sensitive goods, such as weapons or nuclear material, do not accidentally get into the hands of terrorists or enemy nations.

E-commerce

E-commerce—the buying and selling of goods over the Internet— has created new growth in the American economy and provided consumers with the greater convenience of shopping at home, more product choices, and lower prices. However, several problem areas will have to be addressed and regulated by the Department of Commerce if this new segment of the economy is to continue to thrive.

For example, the department must create standards of data protection that will prevent consumers' credit card and personal information from being stolen and misused. It also must decide if goods sold on the Internet should be taxed and at what rate. The department must make sure that copyrighted materials and content, such as books, are not made available on the Internet without the owner's, author's, or publisher's permission. The Commerce Department will have to monitor closely the companies and individuals that sell goods over the Internet to make sure they are not selling counterfeit or stolen goods or violating any other company's copyright. As with traditional commerce

An Amazon.com employee prepares dozens of copies of *Harry Potter and the Order of the Phoenix* for shipping to customers across the country and throughout the world. Amazon.com is an Internet-based seller of books, music, clothes, and consumer goods that has become very popular and taken much business away from traditional stores in towns and cities.

across borders, the department will also try to ensure that no trade barriers exist between countries. Customers in one country should be free to buy goods from suppliers in another country without having to pay a large tax or import fee.

At the same time, as the Department of Commerce seeks to encourage, standardize, and regulate e-commerce, it must not neglect the health of traditional retail establishments. It must help "brick-and-mortar" stores in cities, shopping malls, and town centers to find new ways to appeal to customers and offer extra services that Internet sellers cannot. Because the overall vitality and economic health of the communities in which shopkeepers do business are tied to the fortunes of the shops, traditional commerce must learn to adapt to the Internet revolution and find ways to both coexist and compete with e-retailers.

Telecommunications and Space Commerce

The economic boom of the 1990s was largely driven by telecommunications. This was the decade when cell phones, PalmPilots, pagers, the Internet, home computing, and satellite communications became commonplace features of most Americans' daily lives. These communication- and information-based products will continue to evolve and grow in economic importance as more and more of the world's business is conducted electronically and more and more people are employed in the telecommunications industry.

Because most of this information will someday be relayed by satellites rather than cables, wires, or phone lines, the Department of Commerce will encourage the government and American businesses to expand their current satellite presence in space. Until recently, U.S. communications satellites had dominated space, but they have gradually been joined by those of many other nations. If the U.S. hopes to be a major provider of the world's television and radio broadcast signals, Internet access, cell phone service, space-based scientific research, and climate and navigation information, it will need to remain committed to the research, development, and launch of cutting-edge satellite technology.

A Delta rocket carries four communications satellites into space in 1999. Once in orbit, these satellites would help provide wireless telephone service to parts of the United States, Europe, South America, and South Africa.

Moving Forward Together

Outside of the United States, the Department of Commerce will need to contend with powerful alliances (such as the European Union), changing allegiances (like Russia's new friendliness with Germany), and an ever-evolving world map. It will be crucial for the Commerce Department to undertake the difficult negotiations that will help maintain America's status as a superpower even as it works more cooperatively and collaboratively with its trading partners. Above all, the Department of Commerce always needs to remember that its first concern, even ahead of American industries and businesses, is for the well-being of the American people. No amount of business profit will make a nation rich if its citizens are being left behind. The Department of Commerce must ensure that we all move forward together.

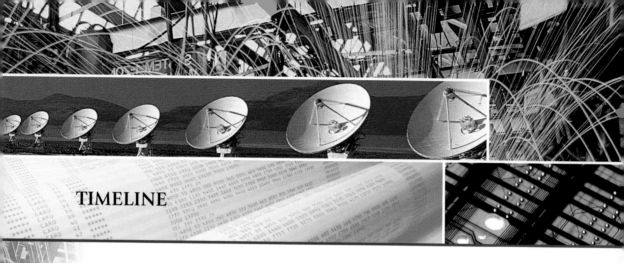

TIMELINE

| 1903 | The Department of Commerce and Labor is created. |

| February 18, 1903–June 30, 1904 | **George B. Cortelyou** |

| July 1, 1904–December 16, 1906 | **Victor H. Metcalf** |

| 1905 | The Bureau of Manufactures is established. |

| December 17, 1906–March 5, 1909 | **Oscar S. Straus** |

| March 6, 1909–March 4, 1913 | **Charles Nagel** |

| 1913 | The Department of Commerce and Labor are split into two separate cabinet-level offices. |

| March 5, 1913–October 31, 1919 | **William C. Redfield** |

| December 16, 1919–March 4, 1921 | **Joshua W. Alexander** |

| March 5, 1921–August 21, 1928 | **Herbert C. Hoover** |

| 1925 | The Patent Office and the Bureau of Mines are transferred from the Department of the Interior to the Department of Commerce. |

| 1926 | The administration of commercial aeronautics is given to the Department of Commerce. |

| 1927 | The Radio Division of the Department of Commerce is created. |

| August 22, 1928–March 4, 1929 | **William F. Whiting** |

March 5, 1929–August 7, 1932 | Robert P. Lamont

August 8, 1932–March 3, 1933 | Roy D. Chapin

March 4, 1933–December 23, 1938 | Daniel C. Roper

1934 | The Federal Employment Stabilization Board is established in the Department of Commerce.

December 24, 1938–September 18, 1940 | Harry L. Hopkins

1940 | The Weather Bureau is transferred from the Department of Agriculture to the Department of Commerce.

September 19, 1940–March 1, 1945 | Jesse H. Jones

March 2, 1945–September 20, 1946 | Henry A. Wallace

October 7, 1946–April 22, 1948 | W. Averell Harriman

May 6, 1948–January 20, 1953 | Charles Sawyer

1949 | The Public Roads Administration is transferred from the Federal Works Agency to the Department of Commerce. The Office of Transportation and the Transportation Council are established.

1950 | The Federal Maritime Board and the Maritime Administration are established in the Department of Commerce.

January 21, 1953–November 10, 1958 | Sinclair Weeks

1955 | The Office of International Trade Fairs is established.

1956 | A major expansion of the federal highway system begins, administered by the Bureau of Public Roads.

November 13, 1958–June 30, 1959 | Lewis L. Strauss

August 10, 1959–January 19, 1961 | Frederick H. Mueller

January 21, 1961–January 15, 1965 | Luther H. Hodges

1961 | The International Travel Service is established.

January 18, 1965–January 31, 1967 | John T. Connor

1965	The Economic Development Administration (EDA) is established.
June 14-1967–March 1, 1968	Alexander B. Trowbridge
March 6, 1968–January 19, 1969	C. R. Smith
1969	The Office of Minority Business Enterprise is established.
1970	The Office of Telecommunications, the National Oceanic and Atmospheric Administration (NOAA), and the National Technical Information Service are established.
January 21, 1969–February 15, 1972	Maurice H. Stans
February 29, 1972–February 1, 1973	Peter G. Peterson
1972	The Office of Business Economics is renamed the Bureau of Economic Analysis.
February 2, 1973–March 26, 1975	Frederick B. Dent
May 1, 1975–February 2, 1976	Rogers C. B. Morton
February 2, 1976–January 20, 1977	Elliot L. Richardson
January 23, 1977–October 31, 1979	Juanita M. Kreps
1977	The Industry and Trade Administration is established.
1978	The National Telecommunications and Information Administration (NTIA) is established.
1979	The Office of Minority Business Enterprise is changed to the Minority Business Development Agency.
January 9, 1980–January 19, 1981	Philip M. Klutznick
1980	The International Trade Administration is established.
January 20, 1981–July 25, 1987	Malcolm Baldridge
1981	The U.S. Travel and Tourism Administration is established.
1982	The Office of Productivity, Technology, and Innovation is established.
1987	The Bureau of Export Administration is created.

October 19, 1987–January 30, 1989 | C. William Verity

1988 | The Technology Administration is established to promote the nation's economic competitiveness.

January 31, 1989–January 15, 1992 | Robert A. Mosbacher

1990s | Thanks to a wave of technological innovations in computing and telecommunications, the American economy records the longest uninterrupted period of economic expansion in its history. Though it accounts for only 5 percent of the world's population, the U.S. is responsible for 25 percent of its economic output.

February 27, 1992–January 20, 1993 | Barbara H. Franklin

January 22, 1993–April 3, 1996 | Ronald H. Brown

1995–1999 | Due to the Internet and the changes it has brought to business strategies and investment, the growth in American productivity is double the growth rate of 1969–1995.

April 12, 1996–January 21, 1997 | Mickey Kantor

January 30, 1997–July 19, 2000 | William M. Daley

July 21, 2000–January 19, 2001 | Norman A. Mineta

2000 | The Department of Commerce publishes *Digital Economy 2000*, its report on the Internet's effect on the U.S. economy.

January 20, 2001–February 3, 2005 | Donald L. Evans

2003 | The Digital Freedom Initiative is established. Its goal is to promote global economic growth by transferring the benefits of information and communication technology to entrepreneurs and small businesses in the developing world.

February 7, 2007 | Carlos M. Gutierrez

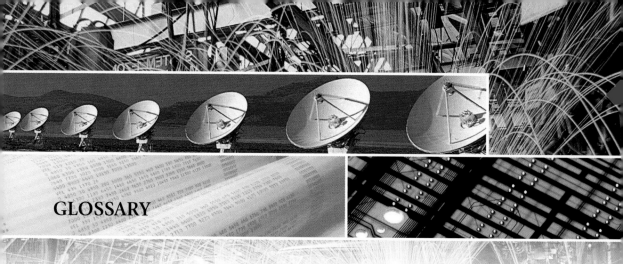

GLOSSARY

commerce The buying and selling of goods.

distribution The act of giving something away, sending something out to various people, or sending something to several destinations.

economy The flow of money within a country, state, region, city, town, or household.

federal The central governing authority in a nation made up of several states or territories.

innovation The introduction of something new and improved; a new idea, method, or device.

manufacturing Making products by hand or machine from raw materials.

monopoly An industry or product that is controlled by only one company.

statistics Information that is collected, counted, analyzed, and presented publicly; information that is collected so that the understanding of a certain issue can be increased.

tariff An extra tax or charge placed upon imported (and sometimes exported) goods.

trusts A group of companies that join together to reduce competition and set fixed and often high prices on their products.

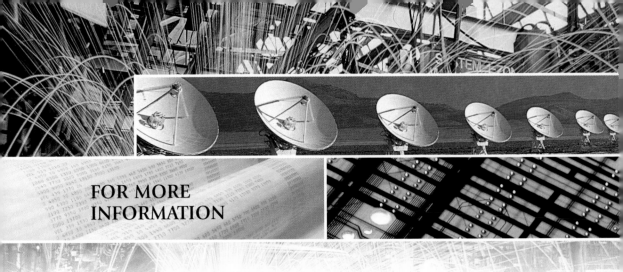

FOR MORE INFORMATION

Bureau of Economic Analysis
1441 L Street, NW
Washington, DC 20230
Web site: http://www.bea.gov

Census Bureau
4700 Silver Hill Road
Washington, DC 20233
Web site: http://www.census.gov

**National Institute of Standards
    and Technology**
100 Bureau Drive, Stop 3460
Gaithersburg, MD 20899
Web site: http://www.nist.gov

National Technical Information Service
5285 Port Royal Road
Springfield, VA 22161
Web site: http://www.ntis.gov

**National Telecommunications
    Information Administration**
1401 Constitution Avenue NW
Washington, DC 20230
Web site: http://www.ntia.doc.gov

Patent and Trademark Office
Crystal Plaza 3, Room 2C02
P.O. Box 1450
Alexandria, VA 22313
Web site: http://www.uspto.gov

U.S. Department of Commerce
14th Street and Constitution Avenue, NW
Washington, DC 20230
Web site: http://www.commerce.gov

WEB SITES

Due to the changing nature of Internet links, the Rosen Publishing Group, Inc., has developed an online list of Web sites related to the subject of this book. This site is updated regularly. Please use this link to access the list:

http://www.rosenlinks.com/tyg/comm

FOR FURTHER READING

Berger, Melvin, and Gilda Berger. *Round and Round the Money Goes: What Money Is and How We Use It.* Nashville, TN: Ideals Children's Books, 2001.

Feinberg, Barbara Silberdick. *The Cabinet.* Breckenridge, CO: Twenty-first Century Books, 1997.

Haywood, John, ed. *Work, Trade, and Farming Through the Ages.* London, England: Lorenz Books, 2001.

Henderson, Harry. *Pioneers of the Internet.* San Diego, CA: Lucent Books, 2001.

Holford, David M. *Herbert Hoover.* Berkeley Heights, NJ: Enslow Publishers, Inc., 1999.

Horn, Geoffrey M. *The Cabinet and Federal Agencies.* New York, NY: World Almanac, 2003.

Maestro, Betsy. *The Story of Money.* New York, NY: Clarion Books, 1993.

Mattern, Joanne. *From Radio to the Wireless Web.* Berkeley Heights, NJ: Enslow Publishers, Inc., 2002.

Pfiffner, James P. *Understanding the Presidency.* New York, NY: Pearson Longman, 2002.

Wellman, Sam. *The Cabinet.* Broomall, PA: Chelsea House Publishers, 2001.

Wilson, Anthony. *Communications.* New York, NY: Larousse Kingfisher Chambers, 1999.

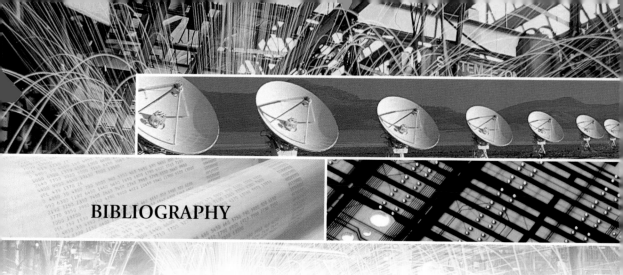

BIBLIOGRAPHY

"About the Bureau of Industry and Security." Bureau of Industry and Security. September 2003. Retrieved September 2003 (http://www.bis.doc.gov/about/index.htm).

Abramson, Rudy. *Spanning the Century: The Life of W. Averell Harriman, 1891–1986.* New York, NY: William Morrow, 1992.

"Commerce History." Department of Commerce. May 2003. Retrieved September 2003 (http://www.commerce.gov/history.html).

Culver, Henry A. *American Dreamer: A Life of Henry A. Wallace.* New York, NY: W. W. Norton & Company, 2001.

"Economics and Statistics Administration Mission." Economics and Statistics Administration Home Page. September 2003. Retrieved September 2003 (http://www.esa.doc.gov/mission.cfm).

"Henry Wallace, 1888–1965: Politician." History Central, 2002. Retrieved September 2003 (http://www.multied.com/bio/people/hWallace.html).

Nash, George H. *Life of Herbert Hoover: The Humanitarian.* New York, NY: W. W. Norton & Company, 1988.

"NTIA Facts." The National Telecommunications and Information Administration. May 1998. Retrieved September 2003 (http://www.ntia.doc.gov/ntiahome/ntiafacts.htm).

Wilson, Joan Hoff. *Herbert Hoover: Forgotten Progressive.* Chicago, IL: Waveland Press, 1992.

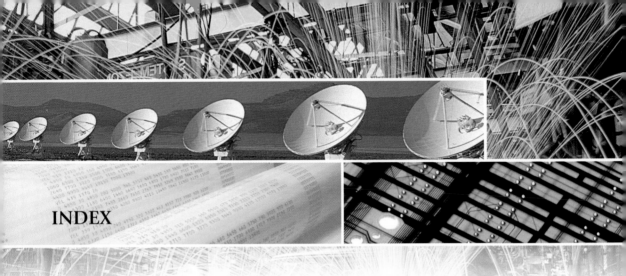

INDEX

LONDON PUBLIC LIBRARY
20 EAST FIRST STREET
LONDON, OHIO 43140

ABOUT THE AUTHOR

Jan Goldberg is an experienced educator and the author of more than fifty nonfiction books and hundreds of educational articles, textbooks, and other projects.

PHOTO CREDITS

Cover and portraits, pp. 29, 43 Department of Commerce; p. 8 NOAA; p. 1 (top and bottom), p. 3 (radio satellites) © Digital Vision/Industry and Technology; p. 3 (document), pp. 4–5 © PhotoDisc Volumes/Business and Occupations; p. 13 © Bettmann/Corbis; p. 17 Library of Congress Prints and Photographs Division; p. 19 © Swim Ink/Corbis; p. 25 © Lee Snider/Corbis; p. 32 © AP/Wide World Photos; p. 37 © AP/Wide World Photos/Chao Soi Cheong; p. 46 © Reuters NewMedia Inc./Corbis; p. 50 © Paul A. Sounders/Corbis; p. 52 © AP/Wide World Photos/Debra Reid; p. 54 © AP/Wide World Photos/Boeing Corp., Carleton Bailie.

Designer: Evelyn Horovicz